Get It!

Understanding the Job Market and Getting the Best Offers

Patty DeDominic

www.thenewnewworldofwork.com

Published by
DeDominic & Associates
2353 East Valley Road
Santa Barbara, CA 93108
805-565-9967
DeDominic.com

©2011 Patty DeDominic
The Author retains sole copyright to the contributions to this book.

Special thanks to: my research and publishing assistant Matt Laband of DeDominic & Associates for editorial help and cover design. We are grateful for contributions to this book by friends and relatives. Grandson Christopher DeDominic Jr. told me which parts were boring and we tried to remove all of that! Carina Steinmetz, filmmaker, former volunteer and intern added her international and youthful perspective.

ISBN #978-1463716226

Dedication

I wrote this book for you! Now that you've proven you can be a great student and you are ready to join tax payer status, congratulations!

Life and the jobs jungle can be a wild ride and I've learned so much in my career as an entrepreneur and head hunter (executive recruiter), and chief executive officer. I paid dearly for this experience and learned over the years how to separate the 95% who "apply for jobs" from the 1-5% who get called back and who actually get the best offers. My advice isn't for everybody. 90% may disagree with me...but the people who apply my advice will increase their offers and pay very quickly.

We hope you enjoy and that you will share this book and empower others too.

Patty DeDominic

Foreword

This book will increase your hire-ability immediately out of school. We aren't going to tell you WHAT to think, but we would like to help you think more about things that will expedite your learning and that contribute to the triple bottom line. People, Profit and Purpose.

Wouldn't it be nice if you could learn how to get the best offers faster? To evaluate yourself more objectively and effectively? Read and apply this book and launch your career with more confidence and tools to put to good use for yourself and others today.

Are you ready? Ready to invent your future? This book CAN help prepare you for the realities for the job hunt right out of school and beyond. **Get It!**

Patty DeDominic
Coach to High Achievers
DeDominic.com

> "I have just finished my studies and am nervous about finding my first job in this highly competitive market."

Are you or any of your friends in this situation?
Are you ready to build your confidence?
Learn what can set you apart from the crowd?
Understand what employers are really looking for?

If you answered 'YES' then this book is for you.

Graduates Ask:

"How long will it take me to find a job?"

"How can I put myself out in front of the competition?"

"How do I get called back for interviews?"

"How do I get better offers?

I'll answer these questions here. I started and built a successful Los Angeles based recruiting firm. For over twenty years we heard and answered these questions for over one million job applicants. I'm the founder of PDQ Careers and helped grow CT Engineering which we purchased and later sold. During my years as a CEO we placed over 250,000 people and learned what it takes to get hired. Let me give you some new tools and techniques now.

You will be able to tap into time tested Tips for Success. We developed these tip and strategies while working with prestigious clients like Wells Fargo Bank, AutoDesk, the Microsoft Corporation, the Auto Clubs, the American Red Cross, AT&T, USC, Universal and Paramount Studios, children's hospitals and governments.

The 7 Things You Need to Know!

Your Network = Your Net-worth

References – Life Long

Looking for a Job is a Full Time Job

Social Media Counts

New Jobs are Invented Daily

Job Clubs – Yes!

Price Matters – Volunteer & Internships Pay Off

Key Skills & Values for 2020

Resiliency

Creativity

Resourcefulness

Integrity

Perpetual Learner

Vision Holder

Light Shiner

Ability to Live With Rapid Change and Ambiguity

GETTING GOOD JOB OFFERS

Getting good job offers is like accomplishing most other goals, except it's harder.

Because it's so personal, it's harder to be objective about it. Being objective as well as professional in your job search is important today. I want to help you unlock your personal power. Yes, your power is in there…waiting for you to shine your light and show off your talents.

Are you ready?

I remember my first job hunt. It was frustrating and confusing, though eventually it was successful.

Maybe you are like me. When I was a teenager I was just hoping someone, anyone, would hire me. I just couldn't wait to get out there and talk to people, to find the lucky person who would become my employer. For weeks it seemed there were no takers!

When I started in the job hunting game for the first time as a 16 year old, it seemed so unfair that all the employers wanted experience. How was I supposed to get experience if employers were only hiring people with experience? It was a Catch-22.

My friends got hired, why didn't I get those offers too? I had some lessons to learn and plenty of doors to knock on. I didn't give up even though each no offer or no openings seemed like a personal rejection. Ouch!

Luckily, someone eventually did hire me. Mrs. DeWeese and Mrs. Opotowski were willing to give me the chance I needed. I learned a lot from these wonderful women, even if I was "just" their babysitter. First jobs, no matter what they are can make a lifetime impact and can teach valuable life lessons. These two women were model moms and homemakers. I got to help them and they helped me refine my ideals and learn working skills.

Fast-forward 30+ years. Plenty has changed, but the enduring principles of success have not.

My goal in writing this is to help you leverage your wondrous, hopeful and optimistic mind set; and enable you to go out and get the jobs you dream about!

You'll soon employ new brain and attitude "muscles" and learn new skills. You may have dreamed of a graduation and being out of school but your next chapter really just begins here! Welcome to the New World of Work. Welcome to tax payer status, I hope you'll shine your light and enjoy this ride of your lifetime.

Recipe for Job Success*

3 parts Willingness to Learn & Grow
3 parts Hard Work
2 parts Contemporary Skills & Experience
2 parts Ability to Communicate & Focus
2 parts "Developing your Network"
1 part Personal Inventory/Self Awareness
1 part Luck

Mix ingredients and let sit, but not for too long. Proceed with your job hunt. Tweak recipe as needed for your dream job and geography.

Add mentors & go!
Apply yourself furiously
Focus on your dream job and your professional goals and daily action plans

VOILA! Job Success! You've Got It!

*Implementation & execution time may vary.
Do try this at home.

You can put this recipe to work immediately. When you use it strategically it will enhance your earning power and your life.

So, go ahead, get ready to take a closer look at yourself. But don't get too comfy. This book is meant to be read while standing, or better yet, while on the run! You will need to get polished up a bit...rev up your enthusiasm, bolster your confidence and shine your own light! Start out by lining up some help for yourself. You are not in this alone, and it's much more fun to share your successes and learnings with others.

Build A Team to Land Great Opportunities

It's going to take a team. As your career launches, and your network grows you are now building a lifeline and support network. You can call this your own personal job lead pipeline and you'll soon fill it with people who can help you. Add people you can help in return. This is an important part of shining your light, sharing your gifts and growing your career. It's one of your success recipes.

Test this and you will soon see if you are half-baked or ready to go! We want to help you become fully baked (meaning competitive and job ready). Not only able to get job offers, but being able to add real value to your own pipeline and that of others. This keeps you not just employed, but more competitive and in demand.

Today's Employers Want to *Have Their Cake* and *Eat it Too*! Are you done or only half-baked?

"Fully baked? How will I know when I am ready? I was hoping to be already 'done'!"

You will know when you are ready because people will refer job leads to you. Offers will start coming in as soon as you begin to unlock your personal power. The better prepared you are, the more options you will have. Let me show you how to 'get lucky' at this game called the Job Hunt.

Job Hunting 101 Checklist

I created a short Job Hunting Checklist. This will help you gauge how much homework you will have. Each person has his or her own criteria for a satisfactory job. No matter what yours is, you can increase your options and *Get It* faster.

Give yourself one point for each check mark. Most people score 5 or less when they make their first call or email to get an interview. If you score 7 or less, you have your work cut out for you. If you score 8-9 then you can be ready in two days or less. If you score 10, congratulations! You are well on your way to successful job offers.

Job Hunting 101 Checklist

Check all that apply:

- ☐ Resume & Cover Letter
- ☐ Resume & Cover Letter Proofread
- ☐ References Prepared
- ☐ Computer Skills Updated
- ☐ Transportation Arranged
- ☐ Prepared and Able to Work
- ☐ Strengths and Weaknesses Defined
- ☐ Proper Attire for the Job
- ☐ Attitude Adjusted and Focused
- ☐ Mentors or Job Counselors
- ☐ Elevator Pitch Ready

Tally Your Score: _____

Checklist Assessment

After reviewing your job readiness have your mentors or friends/parents rate you on the **Job Hunting 101 Checklist**.

How well do you know yourself?_____
_____
_____

How does your score compare to the score they gave you?_____
_____
_____

Do you have work to do?_____
If so, list what:_____
_____
_____
_____

Do your mentors know you any better after this exercise?_____

If not, why not?_____
_____
_____

If yes, congratulations! You can help us write the next book!

Q:

What are the
key steps
in the
successful job hunt?

A:

Prepare Yourself.

1. Plan your approach

2. Identify your preferred industry, locale and job

3. Talk to people already there, get their advice

4. Check help wanted and company mission on their website

5. Apply

6. Follow up & send Thank you!

7. Reel in the offers

8. Close the deal, Get It!

9. Start the job and deliver value everyday!

10. Learn a lot and have fun

Q:

**Where
do
I
*start?***

A:

Warm referrals are the best!

Ask the company you have interned with, as well as your friends and local business people for referrals.

Some of our favorite sources for "cold" job leads are on the Internet, such as Craigslist. You will find thousands of jobs on-line. We are also seeing notices posted in store windows and on company websites. Job openings are everywhere. Learn to mine them to find your gold and don't forget to share some of the leads with your network of friends. Helping a fellow student now might help you later in life. *Paying it forward pays off!*

Update your LinkedIn, Facebook and BranchOut profiles and ask for recommendations. Check to make sure your LinkedIn, BranchOut and other social media sites are consistent with a professional image of someone hireable.

Q:

How long will this *job hunt* take?

A:

How *fast* can you learn?
How *flexible* are you?

Some people get call backs and job offers their first day out. Others may take weeks or even months to customize their approach. One thing for sure, you will get signs of your job suitability immediately.

The time span of your first job hunt depends on the types of jobs you are going after. Ask people already employed in your target industry or company how long it took for them. You can speed up your process by expanding your list of companies and applying for more jobs each week in related fields or nearby communities. Think out of the box and go Get It!

We Live in a 24/7/365 *Wired World.*

Today's employers have global options and 24-hour availability of support. The far-reaching recessions of the past few years turned the "old" ways of job hunting upside down! That's why I remind you the economy and jobs scene is reinventing itself right now. Most business schools and futurists agree that more than half of the jobs of 5 years in the future haven't even been invented yet! There really is a whole new world of work (almost weekly!).

Your speed of offers depends on many variables including your geography, pay, skills and your competition. Your attitude, self-motivation and actions will speed your job hunt.

Q:

Aren't some people *just luckier* **at this game?**

What part does *luck play*?

A:

Luck does play a part in job search success.

We want you to be able to increase your luck. Your success depends on how qualified, prepared and focused you are. Some people think that others have better luck in job hunts. We know you make lots of your own luck and the more focused and prepared you are, the luckier you get!
    Learn about and polish up your unique gifts. Don't be afraid to share your passion and let your light shine! You are the beacon of luck and light.

Q:

I'm intimidated by the *job-hunting process* Any advice in a nutshell?

A:

Enjoy the journey.

If you prepare yourself and make the decision to be proactive, you'll soon get good job offers. The job hunt is a wonderful opportunity to learn and connect with some great new people.

1. Assemble your necessary documents*, meet with counselors or career coach.

2. Create and review your elevator pitch (see next page) – your "brag sheet."

3. Research job leads and do outreach. Connect and follow up, it is not enough to just apply.

4. Apply on-line and in person every day. It is a numbers game so keep your pipeline full. Make ten career related calls every day!

5. Every action and interview is a learning opportunity.

6. Follow up and send a thank you!

Documents may include resume, diplomas, non-confidential work samples, certificates, letters of reference, social security and identity or legal right to work papers.

Q:

What is an
Elevator Pitch?

A:

Your 30-60 second *upbeat introduction.*

It's your short story which can be used whenever you meet new people. Think of what you might say in the time it takes to ride up to the 10th floor. Practice in front of the mirror and for friends until it sounds great. Keep it real.

One might go like this:

"Hi my name is Jane Smith, I recently graduated from _____ with a degree in marketing. I am looking for a job that will utilize my experience in creating web based content. I hope to find a career that will enable me to pursue my passion for communication and contribute to a companys' mission of reinventing healthcare." (or education or science or...)

Q:

Why would
any company want
my *skills* and me?

A:

Technology is constantly changing the career landscape. Updated and *new skills* are always in demand!

Take a personal inventory of your skills, education and qualities. Think about your unique educational experiences and accomplishments.
Launch your courage, and without being too boastful, make a list of ways you can contribute. Know that employers are likely to be interested in confident, hopeful employees. Enterprises need good employees and collaborators who will help them serve their clients. We all need to stay ahead of the global competition and make money. Your part will be to demonstrate how you can do that for your employer!

Q:

What are today's employers *really* looking for?

A:

There really is no *ONE RIGHT* answer to that question, each employer is unique.

There are some fundamentals that almost all employers agree on:

- Ready and willing to work
- Clean, well-groomed appearance
- Good work ethic
- Be clear and concise
- Be respectful and polite
- Optimistic and can do attitude!
- Low maintenance personality
- Contemporary skills and mind set
- Work well with others
- Good cultural fit
- Bottom line: people who add value to the company.

Q:

How can I *stand out* from other job hunters?

A:

Shine your *unique lights* and show off your talents.

You have a set of characteristics and skills that can make you stand out. It is also helpful to recognize the strengths and weaknesses of individuals in your chosen profession/industry. If you can identify those things, then it becomes much easier to recognize how you differ.

Interviewing is a good way to make you stand out from the rest of the applicants. Keep a positive attitude, be energetic and lively, do not speak in a monotone voice, and demonstrate that you are a motivated go-getter.

Avoid sob stories, it is a tough job market and economy for everyone. Employers really don't want to hear about the hardships you have been facing in your employment search or personal life. This is a professional interview, do not get too personal.

"Try to stand out from all others; find what your unique strength is and then use it to be innovative. Employers like innovative employees who think about what extra they can do, not just what they have been told to do."

Jim Delshad
CEO, American International Business Technology, Inc.
Mayor of Beverly Hills (2011)

Q:

How much *follow up* should I do?

A:

Persistence has a positive effect in almost *any endeavor.*

Use good judgement for each potential employer, but don't be afraid to "GO FOR IT" if you feel you can contribute to an employer's company and mission. Most applicants will simply give up when they receive a rejection, however the truly determined will press on.

If you are not chosen for a position, write back with thanks. Ask that they keep your Resume on file if something should come up, and if they could recommend you.

Perhaps that employer hired someone who is not working out. Your optimistic, enthusiastic follow up and sincere thanks and expression of continued interest could pay dividends.

"Be persistent, follow your heart. You spend a great deal of time at work, so be sure to choose an industry you enjoy and a company you respect. If you don't succeed in capturing the attention of a company you like, don't give up. Try creative approaches to get their attention. Persistence usually pays off."

Paul Orfalea
Founder and former Chair of the Board, KINKO's

Q:

How valuable are my *computer and Internet research skills?*

A:

Internet literacy is todays *gold*.

Make technology and the Internet your friend, leverage your technological skills to your advantage. Proclaiming you are a technophobe or hate social networking will not help you!

Your ease in navigating search engines, social networks and the gaming world can be turned into your advantages. Jobs like bloggers, web gardners or masters and social media managers did not exist a decade ago. As of today, YouTube and Google are the most popular search engines.

What are you doing to enhance your web presence? With your supervisors blessing, you can help your employer increase their image in ways which reinforce the company mission.

Q:

How can I continue to develop *my skills?*

A:

Spend time with *mentors, research* and *read the news*!

Talk to your mentors about trends in your industry. You can search the Internet for journals, online classes and webinars. Do all you can to hone and learn new skills, this will build up your confidence and eventually your pay.

A recent Google search netted over 200 accredited schools offering both degrees and training.

There are other alternatives available, such as Lynda.com – one of the fastest growing educational companies in the United States.

Q:

Can I use *Government resources?*

A:

Absolutely!

Visit your local Employment Development Department (EDD) or the One Stop for job listings and coaching. Your local EDD gives access to job listings, feedback on your resume, can review your skill sets and include you in support groups. Most offer summer jobs programs and referrals to paid or unpaid internships.

Most 'government grants' will come in the form of job counseling & EDD workshops. There are also valuable tax credits provided to employers in certain areas and populations.

The U.S. Department of Labor website can direct you to the One Stop in your state. Billions of tax dollars have been invested in this resource - use it to your advantage. www.dol.gov/dol/jobs.htm.

In California, you can find this resource at www.caljobs.ca.gov.

Q:

What about extra curricular activities? Do they help?

Beware of pity parties!

A:

Become part of a *network of people* who help and refer job leads to each other.

    Your college career center will have lots of resources for you and most offer free counseling and job referrals, use it and a strong network to help you fill your prosperity pipeline. Many interviewers place a lot of weight on referrals from people they trust. Most people have heard of the hidden job market. Hiring data shows that referrals, not classified ads, are responsible for over 80% of new job starts.

    Your network is often directly connected to your net worth. Even if you don't aspire to become rich, learn to build a quality network. Enrich it and your network will better nurture you!

    Invest in yourself by making plenty of pay-it-forward deposits. Think alumni connections, your church, professional associations and conferences. Tend your "in-person' and online networks and they can return dividends a plenty.

Neon Signs
and
Silver Platters

Don't wait for flashing lights, neon signs or silver platters for your best opportunities. Find and pursue opportunities everywhere!

Q:

With employers asking us to apply online *are resumes* **and** *cover letters* **really needed?**

A:

Your Resume
is your calling card
make it a good one!

Keep your resume updated, online and printed on nice paper. Your resume is often your "admission ticket." Like a driver's license or passport, you'll need to produce one when asked for it.

Always customize your cover letter to the company you are applying to, never use a boilerplate form letter. The effort (or lack of) shows and does make a difference.

You can also find free resume help online by Googling for 'free resume help' or at www.pongoresume.com or my website www.dedominic.com.

Q:

**What
are
Keywords?**

A:

Keywords are terms *frequently used* in your *job or industry.*

Use Keywords in your skill based or chronological resume. Examples are software programs, social media, scientific and industry specific terms as well as special qualifications and certifications.

Recruiters rely on technology to sort through thousands of leads and are looking for specific skills, people and employers. They search for keywords to find your resume. Understanding and highlighting your special skills increases your hits.

Remember to list those valuable skills on any applications you fill out. Even if you learned some technical or specialized skills while in internships or volunteering, list them. Proof read your resume and have a trusted friend, mentor or academic professional review it before sending it out.

Q:

Is it truly
dog eat dog
and everyone for themself
in this job market?

A:

It does not pay to be a *Lone Ranger* in the job hunt game, Be a *transformer*!

Today's workplace leverages teams of people organized around projects, much like the movie-making process. People have their specialties and must be able to work independently AND collaborate in teams.

Planting the seeds of opportunity starts with being a friend to others and cultivating strong alliances. Build and use your own success team to help in your job hunting. Four eyes can see more than two, twenty eyes and ears keeping their radar tuned for job leads will end up finding lots of opportunities.

Look for job hunting friends and mastermind groups (though be careful not to join or become a 'sorry club') – teams pay dividends. You never know when you might need someone.

Q:

Should I focus on
job interviews
or
temporary employment?

A:

Both!
Sometimes temping is used as a trial to see if a long-term fit will work.

It is common for some companies to use a pay-rolling service for new staffers during a trial period. In the new world of work your income opportunities could come in many forms; employee, temporary worker, or freelancer.

Make the most out of each temp job, volunteer opportunity or internship by meeting people who are successful there. Learn what to do and what not to do by observing what works most effectively.

Q:

How many *interviews* will it take?

A:

There is no *magic number:* go on lots of interviews.

    The more you "audition" for your future leading role, the faster you will Get It!
    Constantly find places to interview. As you get better you will increase your experience and confidence. You will also get some good feedback. Employers try to avoid desperate people. Try to show that you are interested and that you are considering other opportunities too. Each interview gets you closer to your goals.
    Keep a job log of places you have applied to and follow up with the best opportunities. Stay upbeat, always be optimistic and eager, but never appear desperate. Practice confidence building techniques to perfect yourself and your "elevator pitch." Send plenty of thank you notes.

Q:

How can I be as *Competitive* as possible?

A:

Learn as much as you can about industries and companies that interest you.

Your mentors can help inform your about the industry! Talk to as many people as you can in your chosen job or field. Ask your faculty members, parents, counselors and even your coach(es) for advice. People love to be asked bugged or begged - Not! But consulted, yes!

Don't be afraid to ask to do an informational interviews. An informational interview is one which gathers general facts, makes friends, and increases your network.

In addition, apply for specific job openings. Learn as much as you can about what is valued in this particular company. What is their mission? Read the company website and wikipedia and use this information to formulate relevant questions. How does this company perceive value? Ask and answer these and you are halfway there.

Find videos online at www.lynda.com. There are many free audio and video recordings produced by successful professionals talking about their work and their passions. Take advantage of this rich source for preparation.

Q:

I'm desperate for a job. Should I take the *first paying offer* I receive?

A:

Yes,
if it *fits*
with your *goals*!

Some say it is easier to land your next job when you are currently employed. You should accept the offer when it fits well with your long or short term goals.

Ask lots of questions. If you have done your homework, your research about the company and the job, you are more likely to recognize good opportunities when you see them.

I do caution about simply accepting "the first job offered" if the fit isn't right. This will work against you in the long run. Changing jobs too often, without a great reason or a fabulous new opportunity, will damage your professional reputation.

"Follow the interests of your mind and heart. Then work, work, work."

Henrietta Holsman Fore
President Holsman International
Former Director of the United States Mint,
U.S. Treasury Department

Q:

In such a *volatile economy*, how can I ensure my *job security*?

A:

You Can't!
Strive for employability,
keep on learning.

Read more and stay abreast of your industry news and trends. Doing related volunteer work can help you stay fresh & build your network.

You can find needed information in a variety of places. Sources of data on your preferred job can be found on US Department of Labor, at trade associations, and at your Chamber of Commerce, on experts' blogs and news online.

Employers often post skill requirements on their website. If you are in school, your career center office or library will have reference materials for you.

The Department of Labor website has information such as average wages, number of hires in each occupation by region, state and across the country. Visit www.dol.gov.

Simply showing up isn't enough. Focus and a commitment to continually renewing your skills is essential for staying employed.

"Employers need qualified people with the ability to change with the business environment. Maintaining a strong positive attitude is a key to a successful career. Listening to the needs of the business and developing skills to meet future requirements of the company will make you invaluable."

Robert T. Bouttier
Automobile Club of Southern California

Q:

What is the best *resume type* for me?

A:

That depends on your industry *and* your skill sets.

Recent graduates are best served with a traditional education based resume when applying right out of school. However, if special skills or certifications were acquired during your education make sure to list those as special skills and keywords. Your internships and volunteer projects matter too.

LinkedIn and BranchOut are living, virtual resumes that need regular maintenance. Don't forget them. Many employers and recruiters rely heavily on these tools when head hunting.

We live in a digital keyword world, so it pays to be a bit of a keyword name dropper in your profile and resume. Don't be a deceiver, honesty and integrity count!

Patty's Best Resume Tips

1. After you have done some soul searching and promised you will avoid politically correct BS, do write a REAL JOB objective.

Personalized for the actual organization you are applying to, For example, if you apply to the Jane Goodall Institute, your Objective could look like this: Objective: To join a team of people committed to environmental and animal preservation which is doing work around the world. If you are applying to Genentech, you might say something like: My objective is to work with an innovative health company who believes in integrity, competitively winning and is passionate about making a difference in the world. (Their values, found on that corporations website)

2. Ask your friends and mentors to send your resume to the hiring authority and the CEO or board member of the organization you wish to work for

When HR gets your resume from the CEO's office they pay more attention to it. Since warm referrals are best, you are smart to leverage your network in this way. Using your best judgment, so as not abuse your friends/mentors time, YOU are actually doing them a favor by letting them help you land the dream job. Who wouldn't want to help their real friends or people they mentor?

Patty's Best Resume Tips

3. Include one or two wonderful testimonials about you by someone who matters to this employer whether you submit on line or snail mail!

If the CEO of Revlon ever said anything wonderful about me, and I was later applying for a job for any other beauty or big consumer company, I would say that the comment by the Revlon CEO would get read. Short Sound bites grab attention...Now you get to interview.

4. Demonstrate what makes you unique and innovative in the opening paragraph of your cover letter.

Employers today need people who can make their points quickly and who will demonstrate regularly that they are innovative and different than the 1,000 other resumes they got today!

5. Remember that your "resume" also lives on line now at Linked In, Facebook, BranchOut and other social media.

Please keep those updated and don't think that writing a new customized resume for a brand new job is enough...when the employer does their due diligence on you, they WILL check out what you said in other places! You will increase your employability tenfold when YOU are focused on what you really want and know how you can actually contribute to the company (instead of being a dependent).

Q:

What do I do about my lack of *paid work experience?*

A:

Use a skills-based resume that features your more in demand skills.

Include a short narrative of your accomplishments. It is common for students, stay-at-home parents or care givers to have employment gaps. Don't be afraid to put all your best traits, skills, and most relevant experiences up front. You can explain gaps if you are asked later.

Be honest and focus on what you feel you can do for the employer. This is a good reason to cultivate strong personal referral networks, which may look at your resume but not rely on it. Who-you-are comes across in these personal referrals, rather than what-you-look-like on paper. Both matter. Don't give up.

Q:

What about
thank you letters?

A:

Send them!

    Please remember to send thank you letters. Email is okay, printed and signed letters are even better. Little courtesies have ripple effects.

    A sincere expression of your gratitude is good business. Even though we now live in a digital age with robots and seemingly impersonal computers, relationships and manners still make a big difference.

    One young man came to turn down his job offer in person. I was so impressed with his gracious sense of professionalism that I called him a year later to offer another even better job opportunity. He couldn't accept that one either, but he referred Matt Laband to me and this helped Matt launch his management and publishing career.

Q:

**Should I try
to be *part-time*
if *full time job* offers
aren't coming in now?**

A:

Part time and *temporary jobs* are a great way to *get your foot in the door.*

You may be able to experience different companies and fields by being more flexible about part time and temp jobs. You may wish to register with both local and virtual agencies.

This is a great way to get a job quickly, enlarge your network and build new skills. It also lets employers see you and "try before they buy." Talk with your staffing firm representative to see if they serve clients and occupations that are a good fit for you.

Extra hint – try to have this conversation face to face, it will help the interviewer remember you! Even the presidency of the United States is a four year 'temp' job!

Q:

How can I *best prepare* for an interview?

A:

Practice makes perfect.

Review the job description, company history and their website with a fine tooth comb. Learn about the mission and values of this employer and consider how it aligns with your passions.

Talk to your mentors and friends who already work there or in the industry. Have your story ready. Be open and courteous while still maintaining a professional demeanor. Look for ways in which you can contribute to the position you are interviewing for.

Treat all interviewers and staff as if they are your most important customer – they may just become that!

Q:

How do I *analyze my skills objectively?*

A:

Ask people in *your network* to *provide objective feedback.*

This is a time to do some personal reflection and to get lots of good input. Choose your coaches and mentors carefully and pay attention to feedback from parents, teachers and mentors. Choose those who have a positive outlook on life for the best source of motivation and inspiration.

Ask yourself what the marketplace is paying for your skills and remember that value is often in the eye of the "customer." The market "votes" for you with job offers. Count your votes and enhance your skills and openness to Get It.

Read professional journals and e-zines, ask your network and your job coach for feedback. Use online resources to analyze your skills at: wikihow.com/Analyze-Your-Skills-and-Job-Options.

Q:

How much *money* should I *expect to make?*

A:

Wages vary depending on *geography, labor supply and skill sets* required.

Generally, medical or technological fields pay more. Do your research to learn about your chosen field and location.

Talk to people who are already working in your desired field. Find competitive pay at your local Employment Development Department, job club or at www.salary.com. You can also do some market research by reading the help wanted job postings online and in the newspapers.

Value experience over the actual wage for the first few years. Set some benchmarks you would like to achieve. Once when you have demonstrated your value, you can earn raises due to your increased contributions.

Q:

How do I know
if I can trust
online resume submission
companies?

A:

Ask your network about how and where they found success.

Getting referrals for resume writers and resume submission companies and agencies or staffing firms is the best way to find a good source for you. Beware of total strangers with income schemes which sound too good to be true. Most likely they are.

If in doubt, call the firm or Google them to get more insight into their general reputation. Use caution and do not send off too much personal information (credit info, etc.) until you know with whom you are dealing. I like Yelp! and other consumer blogs. Balance openness to new people and places with your good judgement and common sense.

Q:

**How can I
avoid falling victim
to fake/fraudulent
job postings?**

A:

If it seems
too good to be true
it probably is.

As online resources become more and more popular with job seekers, so too does the likelihood of encountering fake or fraudulent job postings. It is important to be aware of how to avoid falling victim to these scams; because the consequences can be quite severe. Pursuing fake job postings or scams can result in signing up for an unwanted product or service, or worse identity theft.

If you inquire or apply for a job posting on an Internet job resource and the poster requests things like: a credit check, personal information (Social Security Number, bank account details) or other important information, use extreme caution.

Do your due diligence. Never blindly provide personal information without some assurances you know they are legitimate.

Q:

Should I use a *staffing agency* in my job hunt?

A:

Yes!

Your job search might include reaching out to every potential hiring source or circle of influence. Find the firms which specialize in your location or industry. Register and interview at lots to get more interviewing experience. You will want to show off your exceptional "hire-ability" and practice telling your story or 'elevator speech'.

These intermediaries can be useful for you and should be considered an important part of your circle of resources. They can give you some great objective market intelligence and personal feedback too.

Q:

What are the odds that I'll get a *corporate gig* with *benefits*?

A:

99.7% of all employer firms, employing just over half of all private sector employees, are small businesses.

According to the U.S. Small Business Administration, 64% of net new jobs created in the past 15 years were created by small businesses with sales under $25 million per year.

While small business, education and government account for more jobs than corporate America, you can get a good job with a major corporation and full benefits if you focus your interviews there. Benefits vary considerably in small enterprises. Research as much as you can about an employer before you apply.

Many firms list a menu of employee benefits on their websites and some have very generous packages, which could include education tuition assistance, paid time off, meals, transportation help, medical, dental insurance and retirement assistance.

Q:

Is there another *non-traditional way* for me to get a job?

A:

Networking and *volunteer referrals* are the *biggest source* of *job offers.*

Hiring statistics show that more jobs are filled by referrals from insiders. Many jobs never get posted or advertised. Your friends and family, customers and vendors are a good source of job-hunting intelligence. Good leads and referrals also will come from the big job boards like Monster and your local newspaper, the EDD, your local Chamber of Commerce as well as your church, job clubs or support groups. Volunteers often learn about paying job leads long before they are posted.

Another great source of referrals is your alumni association, school career centers and employment agencies. Leave no stone unturned. Give yourself the best options and the most leads. Look beyond the obvious sources and you will find your leads multiplying.

Q:

I've had a lot of trouble even getting called for interviews. How do I *rebuild* my *confidence*?

A:

Keep on learning, practice your elevator pitch and look for ways to increase your contacts.

Surround yourself with positive people who are also committed to learning new skills.

Start a list of things you are grateful for. It doesn't have to be long…even 3 or 4 items is a good start. Reviewing this list and expanding as you think of other things that gave you pleasure and success will help you list skills you can contribute to your next job.

Get out and get some exercise and some fresh air. When you take a break to "smell the roses" you give yourself a real boost. You can become a miracle magnet by remembering your passions and shining your special lights!

Some quotes are timeless and were reprinted from my first book, The New New World of Work.

Special thanks to:

Paul Orfalea, Fed-Ex Kinkos

Henrietta Holsman Fore, US Mint

Robert T. Bouttier, Automobile Club

Mayor Jim Delshad, City of Beverly Hills

APPENDIX

Great In Demand Skills

Photo Editing: Learning photo editing is an invaluable skill today. There are programs to choose from, but Photoshop is considered by many to be the industry standard.

Blogging: is a popular communication tool. Wordpress is a popular blog development tool, which can be used to create entire websites, it is very intuitive and user friendly.

Outlook Email: the most common email program which allows you to manage mail, contacts and calendar tasks.

Adobe In Design: Is a powerful publishing tool. It can do most anything with regards to document layout and design.

File Sharing: using Google Documents, Go to My PC, GoToMeeting, Dropbox or other methods to share work with others are tools now in daily use.

Microsoft Excel: will enable you to make spreadsheets with tables and is also a basic accounting program.

Film Editing: Filming, editing and publishing videos can all be done digitally now. Understanding the process and becoming familiar with the software used is an invaluable tool for anyone in a creative field.

Job Hunting 101 Checklist

Check all that apply:

☐ Resume Updated
☐ Resume Proofread
☐ References Prepared
☐ Computer Skills Updated
☐ Transportation Arranged
☐ Prepared and Able to Work
☐ Strengths and Weaknesses Defined
☐ Proper Attire for the Job
☐ Attitude Adjusted and Focused
☐ Mentors or Job Counselors
☐ Elevator Pitch Ready

Tally Your Score: _____

Give yourself one point for each check mark. Most people score 5 or less when they make their first call or email to get an interview. If you scored 7 or less, you have your work cut out for you. If you scored 8-9 then you can be ready in two days or less. If you scored 10, congratulations! You are well on your way to successful job offers.

Example Chronological Resume
John Smith
jsmith@email.com
123 Easy Street
Anytown, USA, 93110
805-555-5555

Education
University/College, Anytown, USA
Bachelor of Science
Major: Physical Education   Major GPA: 4.0/4.0   Cumulative GPA: 3.4/4.0
Academic Honors
Dean's List 2 Semesters   Honors Program Fall 20XX – spring 20XX

Related Academic Projects
Weight Reduction and Stress Management Project: worked with a group of volunteer candidates on a weight reduction program that emphasizes stress management techniques.

Career Objective

    To obtain a career as a manager in a health and fitness oriented environment.

Related Experience
    Fitness Instructor   20XX-Present
    University Fitness Center, Anytown, USA
- Assisted instructor with exercise fitness programs (20 hours weekly).
- Led and instructed 27 aerobics participants and integrated exercise data.

    Practicum Experience
    University Wellness Center, Anytown, USA   20XX-20XX
- Coordinated and led group exercises; administered warm up and cool down exercises.
- Assisted with fitness testing and recommended exercise plan.
- Presented educational seminars on stress management.

    Strength and Conditioning Trainer
    Youth Training Center, Anytown, USA   20XX-20XX
- Developed conditioning programs for youth ages 12-17.
- Assisted conditioning coach with supervision of speed and endurance programs and recorded as well as maintained strength and conditioning data.

    Sales Representative
    Jim's Sporting Goods, Anytown, USA   20XX-20XX
- Train new employees in day-to-day operations.
- Responsible for store opening and closing procedures.
- Contribute to increased customer sales through extensive product knowledge.
- Provide superior customer service to patrons.

Certifications and Professional Designations
CPR and First Aid certification, American Red Cross, Anytown, USA   20XX

www.thenewnewworldofwork.com

Example Skills Based Resume
John Smith
jsmith@email.com
123 Easy Street
Anytown, USA, 93110
805-555-5555

Education
University   Anytown, USA
Bachelor of Arts Degree
Major: Sales   Minor: Marketing   Cumulative GPA 3.0/4.0

Career Objective
To obtain a marketing position with an advertising agency that will utilize my sales background and my interpersonal communication skills.

Sales Skills
- Contributed to the increase of the average dollar sale at the retail level through product knowledge, demonstration, and point-of-sale interactions.
- Participated in group oriented project to prepare marketing and promotional materials for advertising for the purpose of recruiting new members into the college's Student Alumni Association.

Communication Skills
- Created and edited press releases for a Pittsburgh-based hospital; composed feature, sports, and editorial pieces for the University student newspaper.
- Conducted weekly meetings and presentations with fraternity representatives and Greek Life Coordinator in preparation for Rush, which involved several hundred students.

Organizational and Managerial Skills
- Handled purchases and returns, and prepared in-store marketing for university bookstore. Trained new employees, performed business transactions.
- Worked directly with Greek Life Coordinator for one year to coordinate and facilitate fraternity rush.
- Effectively acclimated a community of 20 undergraduate freshmen to college life through regular interpersonal and group contact, educational and social programming, and enforcement of college policy.

Work Experience

University Bookstore Sales Department	Anytown, USA	20XX-20XX
University Student Life Resident Assistant	Anytown, USA	20XX-20XX
University Newspaper Writer	Anytown, USA	20XX-20XX
Greek Life Council Member	Anytown, USA	20XX-20XX

www.thenewnewworldofwork.com

Notes & Follow Up Action Steps

Notes & Follow Up Action Steps

Notes & Follow Up Action Steps

Notes & Follow Up Action Steps

Notes & Follow Up Action Steps

Notes & Follow Up Action Steps

Notes & Follow Up Action Steps

Notes & Follow Up Action Steps

Notes & Follow Up Action Steps

Notes & Follow Up Action Steps

Interview Notes

Date	Company Name:	Position	Thank You
	Interviewer:		
Phone:		Follow Up:	
E-mail:		Next Steps:	
Additional Notes:			

Date	Company Name:	Position	Thank You
	Interviewer:		
Phone:		Follow Up:	
E-mail:		Next Steps:	
Additional Notes:			

Date	Company Name:	Position	Thank You
	Interviewer:		
Phone:		Follow Up:	
E-mail:		Next Steps:	
Additional Notes:			

Interview Notes

Date	Company Name:	Position	Thank You
	Interviewer:		

Phone:	Follow Up:
E-mail:	Next Steps:

Additional Notes:

Date	Company Name:	Position	Thank You
	Interviewer:		

Phone:	Follow Up:
E-mail:	Next Steps:

Additional Notes:

Date	Company Name:	Position	Thank You
	Interviewer:		

Phone:	Follow Up:
E-mail:	Next Steps:

Additional Notes:

www.thenewnewworldofwork.com

Interview Notes

Date	Company Name:	Position	Thank You
	Interviewer:		
Phone:		Follow Up:	
E-mail:		Next Steps:	
Additional Notes:			

Date	Company Name:	Position	Thank You
	Interviewer:		
Phone:		Follow Up:	
E-mail:		Next Steps:	
Additional Notes:			

Date	Company Name:	Position	Thank You
	Interviewer:		
Phone:		Follow Up:	
E-mail:		Next Steps:	
Additional Notes:			

Interview Notes

Date	Company Name:	Position	Thank You
	Interviewer:		
Phone:		Follow Up:	
E-mail:		Next Steps:	
Additional Notes:			

Date	Company Name:	Position	Thank You
	Interviewer:		
Phone:		Follow Up:	
E-mail:		Next Steps:	
Additional Notes:			

Date	Company Name:	Position	Thank You
	Interviewer:		
Phone:		Follow Up:	
E-mail:		Next Steps:	
Additional Notes:			

Patty DeDominic

Patty started her business at 28 years of age and built one of California's largest employers until she sold it in 2006. Her team successfully placed over 250,000 people in a variety of industries across the country. Her company interviewed over a million job candidates over two decades and they learned what it takes to get the best offers.

DeDominic perfected winning formulas for making higher quality job placements. The companies she worked with were very successful: PDQ Careers and CT Engineering, developed a strong reputation for extraordinary commitment to people, integrity and professionalism.

Today Patty is an entrepreneur, an investor in diversified companies and social enterprises and a publisher. She and her husband live in Santa Barbara, California. Together they have raised five children and now have five grandchildren.

Made in the USA
Charleston, SC
20 July 2011